The Spanish Inquisition

THE
SPANISH
INQUISITION

Rev. Sydney F. Smith

 BooksUlster

First published by the Catholic Truth Society, London, 1892, as part of *Historical Papers*, edited by Rev. John Norris, S.J. This new edition published by Books Ulster in 2017.

ISBN: 978-1-910375-55-6 (Paperback)

Cover image is from an undated drawing by Thomas Rowlandson (1756–1827).

The Spanish Inquisition

BY THE REV. SYDNEY F. SMITH, S.J.

"The Spanish Inquisition" is still an effective cry whenever it is wished to arouse prejudice against the Catholic Church and her children. It is true the cry is not quite as effective now as it was a few decades ago. There has been of late days much more fusion between Catholics and others in the various walks of life, and our fellow-countrymen have come to know us well, both our clergy and our laity, and have been able to judge for themselves what manner of men we are. They do not find us to be of harsher temperament than themselves, less fond of liberty, or less respectful of the due rights of others. And so when reminded of the Inquisition, although perhaps accepting the popular account of its cruelties as unquestionable fact, they prefer to treat the past as history and judge of the present by the present.

It is consoling to mark this increasing disposition to give us credit for what we are. There is certainly no desire anywhere among us to have renewed the harsh methods and punishments of the Spanish Inquisition. But we will go further and claim that the Spanish Inquisition itself was never the horrible thing it is represented in Protestant literature as having been. Let the reader understand exactly the position we take up. We are far from inviting a judgment of acquittal on all its proceedings. We maintain only that the bad name it has acquired in popular estimation is due largely to the gross exaggerations of those who have written against it in an adverse sense, and to the neglect to view it in relation with the notions and methods everywhere current in the days of its existence.

What then are the charges against this tribunal? They may be summarized as follows. It treated beliefs contrary to the established creed, even though conscientious, as crimes of the first magnitude. It punished offenders with the most cruel punishment of fire, and went so far in its inhumanity as to make their dying agonies a religious spectacle for the entertainment of "the faithful," the very Kings, surrounded by brilliant Courts, presiding over the *autos da fé* [1] ("acts of faith") at which the condemned were delivered to the flames. In the excess of its thirst for heretical blood it did not hesitate to sacrifice whole hecatombs in this way: and in order that the number of victims might not run short, it instituted a grossly unfair judicial procedure whereby the accused person had hardly a chance of rebutting the charges against him. The names of his accusers, often his personal enemies, were concealed from his knowledge, and the services of a skilled advocate whom he could trust to act in his interests were denied him. On the other hand, he was submitted to repeated tortures in loathsome cells, until, unable longer to endure the agony, he was driven to disregard future consequences and seek present relief by a confession of guilt, truthful or feigned. Lastly, to intensify the terror of the tribunal throughout the country, arrests were made with the utmost secrecy, and by secret officials, called "familiars" of the court. These mysterious beings would lie in wait for their victim at some unobserved spot, or they would enter his house stealthily under the cover of the darkness, and carry him from his very bed to their underground dungeons. When the family rose in the morning one cherished member was missing. Wife or children might suspect what had happened, but there was no remedy. Probably they would never see him again except once, and then tied to the burning faggot at some future *auto da fé*. It was hardly safe even to mention his name, still less to express regret at his fate. Nor was

---

[1] The Spanish phrase is *auto de fé*. *Auto da fé* is Portuguese, from which nation therefore we must have originally obtained the word.

this all. Should he be convicted, as he was morally certain to be, all his goods would be confiscated, and the family that had been dependent upon him for its maintenance, would be reduced to poverty, as well as branded with perpetual disgrace and suspicion.

Here certainly is a terrible indictment. Well may the people of England shudder at the bare thought of such a system introduced into their free and happy country. But now what are the facts?

It cannot be denied that the doctrine of intolerance was recognized in those days. It was certainly held to be the duty both of the Church and of the State to treat heresy to the Catholic faith as a crime commensurate with treason, and to adopt stringent measures against its propagation. This was a doctrine unquestioned in those days among all parties. Protestants and Catholics alike, in the countries where they had the upper hand, proscribed and punished their opponents. It did not occur to either side that any other course was rational. Surely, they would have said, truth and error are not on equal terms. Truth has rights: it demands to be upheld and promoted. Error has no rights: and is to be repressed and destroyed.

Our Protestant readers will here urge, that although this is true, yet there is this difference between Protestantism and Catholicism, that, whilst the former now recognizes the sacred rights of religious liberty, the latter continues to be as intolerant as ever, and is always itching to persecute. In a certain sense no doubt it is true that Catholics are still and always will be intolerant of error, for their religion is founded on the conviction that God's revelation is not a mere matter of subjective persuasion, but an external fact attested by certain and convincing proofs. No sane person would claim that virtue and vice ought to have equal toleration in the community, and the attitude of manifest truth to manifest error does not differ, in the abstract, in this respect from the attitude of manifest virtue to manifest vice. If Protestants are, in the abstract, advocates of universal toleration, this is because they do not believe in any objective certainty of religious truth. Creed, for them, is matter of opinion, not of certain knowledge.

But although the two parties are necessarily divided *in theory*, when we compare the same two parties *in their practice*, the balance of intolerance, at least in the present day, and indeed in the past also, would seem to be on the side of Protestants: not indeed of Protestants generally, but of that class of Protestants—Exeter Hall Protestants as they used to be called—who are so fond of flinging the Inquisition in our faces. In old days each party assumed that its opponents were not only in error, but in conscious error. Persecution was supposed and expected to have the effect of making them follow their consciences, not resist them. Nowadays we have come to realize more clearly how differently minds are constituted and how possible it is, in the medley of opposing creeds, not to perceive which out of them all is the truth. This realization is general, and is certainly strongly felt by Catholics, who are also moved by other similar considerations to feel a great dislike for all attempts to coerce religious beliefs. The realization seems to be less marked among Protestants of the class just indicated. Consider, for instance, how often when a man becomes convinced of the duty to turn Catholic, Protestant relations and others have no scruples at all in opposing temporal obstacles of the severest kind in his way. And with this contrast the very great reluctance shown by Catholic priests to receive converts into the Church until they have been well instructed and thoroughly realize what they are about.

These remarks have seemed to be necessary in order to remove a prejudice which might otherwise interfere with a fair hearing of the considerations we have to offer in defence, or rather in extenuation, of the Inquisition. It ought now to be clear that the intolerance shown by this tribunal involves no reflexion on the Catholic Church. Viewed historically, it was intolerance accepted by the age as an obvious duty and accepted by Protestants and

Catholics alike. Viewed as a basis of anticipation concerning the future, it cannot be considered to forebode any likelihood of future similar "persecution" of Protestants by Catholics, should the latter, which does not seem likely, return once more to power.

We shall have to confine our attention to the Spanish Inquisition established in the fifteenth century. The Inquisition itself originated as far back as the twelfth century in Southern France, but nowhere and at no time did these Inquisitorial courts indulge in the multitudinous capital convictions chargeable to the later Inquisition in Spain. It is this Spanish Inquisition which has occasioned the popular outcry against the institution, although most Protestants imagine that it was quite as bad in the other Catholic countries. The Roman Inquisition is still existent. As it does not fall within the scope of our subject-matter we must be content to say that all along it was noted for its comparative mildness, and that at the present day its work is to examine and condemn books and propositions at variance with the Catholic faith.

The Jews had in ancient days been far more numerous and influential in Spain than in any other country, and were even credited with a policy of Judaizing the entire Peninsula. They were accordingly much disliked by the Christian populations, who sought to protect themselves by frequent and stringent repressive laws, ecclesiastical and civil, directed against the enemy. It may be mentioned here incidentally that the Popes, such as Alexander II., the friend of Hildebrand, and Honorius III., are found several times interposing and protesting against the cruel treatment to which the Jews became thus subjected. The race, however, evinced its well-known vitality, and in the fourteenth century had acquired important privileges for the preservation of the status of its members, as well as their admission into some of the primary offices of the Government. The results of the persecution through which they had lived had been, on the other hand, most pernicious in producing a class of Jews who were such at heart, although by open profession they had become Christians. These were in league with the open adherents of their national creed, and were the more dangerous because their machinations against the Catholic religion were carried on in the dark. The extent of the evil may be realized somewhat when it is said that not a few of these secret Jews had risen to high ecclesiastical dignities, some even to bishoprics. These and the like advantages of position, obtained by intermarriage with noble families and the possession of great wealth, they were unquestionably using, in the latter part of the fifteenth century, with the determined policy of erecting Judaism on the ruins of Spanish Catholicity and nationality. Here was a very serious danger for the rulers of the country to take into consideration, and they had the clamorous demands of their terrified Christian subjects to urge them on to action. The crisis came when Ferdinand of Aragon and Isabella of Castile were the reigning monarchs. They met it by establishing the "Spanish Inquisition." It is called by this special name because of its distinctive character. But the older Inquisition had existed in Spain, and had still a staff of officials in the Kingdom of Aragon, not, however, in Castile; although Castile, much more than Aragon, was to be the home of the renewed Inquisition now about to commence its harsh career.

In 1478 (or possibly in 1480) the Sovereigns obtained a Bull from Sixtus IV. to establish a tribunal for searching out heretics. In virtue of its authorization, the tribunal was erected at Seville for the entire Kingdom of Castile, and two Dominicans, Miguel Morillo and Juan Martin, were by royal appointment placed over it as royal inquisitors. After a preliminary season allowed for efforts to gain back the heretics by preaching and persuasion, the work of the tribunal commenced in 1481. It began then, as it invariably began its sessions in any part of the country, by proclaiming a period of grace of sixty or more days, a period often prolonged.

All who came forward during such periods and confessed their heresy, even if it were relapse, were reconciled without incurring any severe penance. It is important, now that we have to consider its doings, to remember that the Inquisition never proceeded against the unconverted Jews, but only against those who after having received Baptism had relapsed, openly or secretly, into Judaism. Such persons were called *Maranos*. In 1483, the famous Torquemada, Prior of the Dominican convent of Segovia, was appointed Grand Inquisitor over the whole of Castile, and shortly after the single court at Seville was supplemented by three others at Cordova, Juan, and Villa-Real (afterwards changed to Toledo). Torquemada held office till 1498, when he was succeeded by Diego de Deza, who in turn gave place to the Franciscan Cardinal Ximenez in 1507.

About twenty years later, the Inquisition, continuing to be employed against the Maranos, found another sphere for its activity in the *Moriscos* of Granada. In 1480 war broke out between the Spanish monarchs and the Moors, who having been at one time the dominating race throughout nearly the whole of Spain, still maintained possession of the Kingdom of Granada in the south-east of the Peninsula. The Spaniards conquered after a war of ten years' continuance, the Moors receiving for the time very favourable conditions, which among other things included freedom to retain their national worship. The conquerors did not, however, understand these terms to prevent them from sending Catholic missionaries to preach to their new subjects, and encouraging conversions by the offer of temporal advantages. We are not maintaining that this was a judicious measure. Indeed, experience proved that it was not, that it led to conversions which were far from solid in their character. The immediate effect of the conversions obtained was to excite the anger of the unconverted Moors, who began to persecute the Moriscos, as the converted Moors were called. Eventually the unconverted rebelled, but they were subdued, and then were offered the alternative of either suffering the penalties of treason which they had incurred, or obtaining pardon by passing over to the Christian religion and receiving Baptism. One can understand how this offer could be well-intentioned if only we bear in mind what has been indicated already, that the Spaniards were persuaded that the Moors in resisting the light of Christianity when set before them were resisting the dictates of their consciences. The measure was productive of its natural results, natural as *we* perceive them to be. Many conversions followed, of a more or less imperfectly sincere kind, and afterwards there were continual attempts to apostatize. In fact, the very same difficulty emerged with regard to the Moors and Moriscos, which had been felt over the Jews and Maranos; or rather a worse difficulty, because the two now became fused into one, by the secret sympathy and combined efforts of the two races involved in the same trouble. Hence the application of the Inquisition to the Moriscos (not the Moors) to retain them in the Christian faith. Hefele, however, tells us that it was never employed so extensively or with such severity against the Moriscos as against the Maranos. In 1524 these Moriscos, addressing the newly-appointed Grand Inquisitor, Manriquez, say: "We have always been treated justly by your predecessors, and properly protected by them." Clement VIII. forbade the confiscation of their property, or the infliction of capital punishment upon them for apostacy. We may call the campaign of the Inquisition against the Maranos and Moriscos the first stage in its history. It lasted till the middle of the reign of Charles V.

The second stage of importance began some fifty years later during the reign of Philip II. At this time there was an attempt to introduce Protestantism into Spain, which was resolutely resisted by the Spanish monarchs with the aid of the Inquisition, and Philip, on this account, is wont to be specially identified by Protestants with the cruelties of the tribunal, although they appear to have been less marked in his reign than in the earlier reign of Ferdinand and Isabella.

This second period lasted till the accession of the Bourbons, when the danger from Protestantism was held to have passed by. From that time onwards the activity of the tribunal was much diminished, and was confined, says Balmez, to the repression of infamous crimes and the exclusion of the philosophy of Voltaire. By the end of the eighteenth century the Inquisition was a shadow of its former self, and it was abolished at the commencement of the present century, first by the Bonapartist King Joseph, in 1808, and again, after a short resuscitation on the return of the Bourbons, finally in 1830.

We can now deal with the charges of cruelty against the Inquisition. These are due largely to the wealth of imagination which seems to characterize anti-Catholic polemical writers. They have, however, a basis which might seem trustworthy in a book on the Inquisition written near the beginning of this century by one Antonio Llorente. Llorente was a Spanish priest, who, although probably a Freemason, had from 1789 to 1793, been Secretary-General to the Inquisition at Madrid. When Joseph Bonaparte was placed by his brother on the throne of Spain, and the Spanish people rose with patriotic ardour against the usurpation, Llorente joined the small body of anti-patriots called *Afrancescados*. This is noteworthy, as it reveals the character of the man. On the fall of Joseph he was naturally banished from Spain and took up his residence in Paris. There he wrote his *History of the Inquisition*, with the aid of the official documents he had pillaged from its archives at Madrid whilst he was enjoying the favour of King Joseph. The book is complete in its way; that is to say, it narrates the history of the tribunal from its commencement to its abolition, and gives detailed accounts of the more famous historical processes and *autos da fé*. It is apparent, however, on the surface, how the author exaggerates everything that tells against the Inquisition, and misconstrues all that is in its favour, particularly any action taken in regard to it by the Popes; and one has strong suspicions that he must be omitting altogether a great deal which would materially reduce his indictment. But there is one thing full of significance about this writer. He tells us himself, in his work, "I burnt with his (King Joseph's) approbation all the criminal processes, save those which belong to history by their importance or celebrity, or by the quality of the person, as that of Caranza, and of Macanez, and a few others. But I preserved intact the register of resolutions of Council, royal ordinances, bulls and briefs from Rome, and all genealogies," &c.[2] For such conduct there can be no excuse. As Balmez reasonably demands, "Was there no place to be found in Madrid to place them (the proceedings and documents), where they could be examined by those who, after Llorente, might wish to write the history of the Inquisition from the original documents!" In consequence of this prudent act of barbarism, we are constrained to base our examination of the tribunal almost entirely on the testimony of this biassed witness. Still, even under these disadvantages, we have the means of rectifying the current Protestant notions. We will now consider one by one the charges against the tribunal enumerated above, not, however, necessarily taking them in the order there given.

As to the number of the victims, Llorente gives the following statistics: In the year 1481, 2,000 burnt and 17,000 penanced; in 1482, 88 burnt and 625 penanced; in 1483, 688 burnt and 5,727 penanced; from 1484 to 1498 (that is, under Torquemada), 6,024 burnt and 66,654 penanced; from Torquemada to the suppression of the tribunal, 23,112 burnt and 201,244 penanced. On Llorente's authority these alarming numbers are invariably adopted by anti-inquisition writers, whose readers naturally assume that Llorente took them from the official records in his

---

[2] iv. 145.

possession. In fact, however, they are mere inferences of a very unreasonable kind from three very slight statements of ancient writers, one of whom he grossly misunderstands. Mariana, as misread by Llorente, is supposed to say that in 1481, the year when the Inquisition commenced its proceedings, 2,000 persons were burnt at the stake, and 17,000 others penanced at Seville alone. Another writer, Bernaldez, is made to say that, also at Seville, from 1482 to 1489 (in reality, he says, from 1481 to 1488), over 700 were burnt and 5,000 penanced. And an inscription on the Quemadero (the platform where the condemned were burnt), at Seville, records that from 1492 to 1524 nearly 1,000 were there burnt, and 20,000 abjured their heresy.

Taking Mariana's supposed statement as it stands, for the year 1481, Llorente calculates from Bernaldez an annual average for the years 1482–1489, and from the Quemadero inscription for the entire remainder of the Inquisition's duration, making, that is to say, gradual reductions at intervals to allow for the known growth of leniency as time ran on. These figures by themselves refer only to the one court at Seville. To obtain figures for the other courts, added in course of time, he multiplies those for Seville, after having with a show of generosity, first halved them. Can anything be more untrustworthy than such a computation, assuming, as it does, that the multiplication of tribunals within the same area of jurisdiction involves a corresponding multiplication of condemned persons, and that the number of condemnations has preserved a calculable average through centuries? Nor is this the only vice. Mariana does not say 2,000 were burnt at Seville in 1481. If he did, he would contradict Bernaldez, since, as we have noticed, Bernaldez includes 1481 in his eight years. Mariana (1592) is in agreement with Pulgar, an earlier writer, (1545), who tells us that these 2,000 were burnt during Torquemada's entire time (1484–1498), and that, not in Seville only, but in the various places to which his activity extended.

Mr. Legge, a non-Catholic writer in the *Scottish Review* (April, 1891), has adjusted Llorente's calculations to this rectified reading of Mariana, and his figures may be set down with advantage for comparison with those just given. In 1481, 298 burnt and 5,960 penanced; in 1482, 88 burnt and 625 penanced; in 1483, 142 burnt and 2,840 penanced; from 1484 to 1498, 2,000 burnt and 40,000 penanced. That is, from 1481 to 1498, 2,528 burnt and 49,425 penanced against Llorente's 8,800 burnt and 90,006 penanced. From 1498 onwards, having no means at hand of testing them, Mr. Legge gives a sceptical adhesion to Llorente's figures. Still, even Mr. Legge, through not adverting to Llorente's mistake of a year in his citation of the passage in Bernaldez, has not reduced these initial facts to their true proportion. The year 1481, according to Llorente's system, being the inaugural year of the Inquisition, must claim to itself a very large proportion of the 700 which Bernaldez assigns to the period (1481–8). This would reduce the annual average for the years following from Llorente's (and Mr. Legge's) 88 to about 40, and would involve a consequent reduction in the annual average for subsequent years at Seville and elsewhere.

We have, however, to bear in mind that inferences like these, deducing the criminal statistics of many districts and many centuries from one to two slight data appertaining to a place and time of exceptional severity, are most hazardous. To what extent this is true, will be the better felt if we make a similar inference from a few chance criminal statistics referring to our own country. Hamilton's *History of Quarter Sessions from Elizabeth to Anne*,[3] gives us the gaol returns at Exeter for 1598. In this year the total result of the two assizes and four quarter sessions was the hanging of 74 persons, many for crimes no greater than sheep-stealing. Starting from these facts Sir James Stephen[4] gathers that,

---

[3] p. 31.
[4] *History of the English Criminal Law*, i. 467.

"if the average number of executions in each county were 20, or a little more than a quarter of the number of capital sentences in Devonshire in 1598, this would make 800 executions a year in the 40 English counties." That is 11,200 in 14 years against Torquemada's 2,000 (or 6,024), in the same period, and some reduction on 264,000 executions in a period of 330 years, the duration of the Inquisition in Spain, against Llorente's 23,112 burnt and 201,244 penanced by this tribunal within that time.

Mr. Legge provides, in the article referred to, another instance very much in point, since it deals with an offence kindred to heresy. He cites Mr. Mackay's *Curious Superstitions*,[5] for a computation that in Scotland from the passing of the Act against witches under Queen Mary, an Act due not of course to her helplessness but to the imperious harshness of John Knox—from this date to the accession of the King James I. 17,000 witches were burnt in Scotland, whilst in England 40,000 supposed witches perished in this way between 1600 and 1680, 3,000 during the Long Parliament which undertook its struggle with the Crown in the cause of civil and religious liberty. It would not do to place too much trust in these numbers. Mr. Mackay is a popular writer, not a historian, and sets down without criticism the figures he finds in ancient authors. It does not seem to occur to him that such authors are merely making wild guesses and in no sense relying on accurate statistics. However, we only require one illustration of wild statistics to set against another. Mr. Legge remarks upon these data that, "even supposing the figures are, as one would fain hope, grossly exaggerated, it would appear that the whole number of Inquisition victims would hardly have afforded the witch-hunters of our own land sport for 50 years." Even when we go further and distrust altogether these inferential statistics, whether in Spain, England, or elsewhere, there seems little doubt

---

[5] i. 237.

that the judicial waste of life in England surpassed that in Spain. Witchcraft, it must be remembered, was an offence which in Spain came under the cognizance of the Inquisition, as did many other offences, partaking to a greater or less degree of a religious character, which did not amount to heresy.

The next charge we have to deal with is the mode of execution employed by the Inquisition. The punishment of fire seems to us cruel and revolting. We moderns cannot tolerate the idea of its infliction on any class of offenders. But this was not the feeling of our ancestors, who were undoubtedly, and regrettably, far sterner and harsher than their descendants, yet are not on that account to be condemned *en masse* as a generation of savages. There is plenty of proof that they had tender hearts like our own. The truth is that human nature is so one-sided. We moderns fix our attention on the acuteness of human pain, and perhaps forget somewhat the gravity of crime. The ancients realized less the throbbings of pain in the criminal's body, as indeed they were less impatient of it in their own, but they realized more the outrage of his guilt, and aimed by their severities at preventing its recurrence. Moreover, it would be a great mistake to suppose that the Inquisition alone is responsible for execution by fire. Witches were punished at the stake in England, Germany, &c., and it was not only to ecclesiastical offences that this mode of death was allotted. It was also the English punishment for high treason, in the case of a woman, or if she murdered her husband. In the Carolina, a code drawn up by the Emperor Charles V. in 1532, and considered to be an innovation in the direction of greater leniency towards criminals, it is the punishment for circulating base coin and other offences. In France, too, it was in use for certain civil crimes, among others for poisoning. We have also to remember that ancient justice knew of harsher modes of death even than the stake. On the continent there was the revolting punishment of the wheel, to which the body of the criminal was tied with tight cords, and where, his bones having been broken by severe blows, he was left to linger in his agonies for hours or days, as the case might be, till death came to release him. This was quite a common punishment for simple murder in France till the time of the Revolution. It was in use in Protestant Prussia as late as 1841. Nor has England any cause to boast of her greater mildness. The punishment for high treason was, to be drawn on the hurdle from the prison to the gallows, to be hanged for a while, to be cut down while still living, to undergo a shocking mutilation, and to have the bowels torn out and burnt before the victim's face. His heart was then pulled out and cast into the fire, his body quartered and beheaded, and the parts exposed in five different places to be the food of the birds. In the time of Henry VIII. an Act was passed decreeing that poisoning should be accounted high treason, and punished by boiling to death. And the Chronicler of the Grey Friars writes: "This year (1531), was a cook boiled in a cauldron in Smithfield, for he would have poisoned the Bishop of Rochester, Fisher, with divers of his servants, and he was locked in a chain, and pulled up and down with a gibbet at divers times till he was dead." From Wriothesley's Chronicle we further learn that this punishment was not deemed unsuitable for a woman. "This yeare (1532), the 17th of March, was boyled in Smithfeild one Margret Davie, a mayden, which had poysoned 3 householdes," &c. In the Low Countries on the establishment of Protestant ascendency it was decreed that Balthassar Gerard, the assassin of William the Silent, should have "his right hand burnt off with a red-hot iron, his flesh torn from his bones with pincers in six different places, that he should be quartered and disembowelled alive, that his heart should be torn from his bosom and flung in his face, and finally that his head should be cut off."[6]

If the Inquisition is to be condemned so severely for not

---

[6] Motley's *Rise of the Dutch Republic*, iii. 612.

emancipating itself from the ideas of its age in the matter of harsh punishments, at least it should receive credit for not having resorted to these refinements of cruelty which were abounding everywhere around it. It was not even primarily responsible for the selection of the fire, as its peculiar mode of execution. The assignment of this punishment to heresy was the State's, not the Church's, choice. The Church handed the heretic over to the secular arm to be punished according to the law of the land. Protestant writers sneer at this distinction, but it is real. The Inquisitors might perhaps have scented heresy in the civil authorities, had they neglected to punish the condemned heretics, and of course they knew what the legal civil punishment was. But there is no ground for supposing they would have opposed themselves violently to any general scheme for the mitigation of the mode of punishment.

We must bear in mind also another fact if we are to estimate the large number sent to the stake at their right value as an index of the disposition, cruel or temperate, of the Inquisitors. Great efforts up to the last moment were always made to induce the condemned to acknowledge his errors and recant. Llorente himself, in the statistics he gives of several *autos da fé*, shows that the proportion of those who recanted to those who persisted in their heresy was large. When the recantation came after relapse it did not usually procure remission of the death-sentence, but it always procured a material alleviation of its severity. The condemned were in that case first strangled, and not till life was extinct were the bodies committed to the flames.

But, it will be said, how vain to seek to exculpate the Inquisition from the charge of savagery, when the *autos da fé* at which the victims perished at the stake in vast numbers at a time were treated as religious spectacles, appropriate for days of festal gathering, presided over by ecclesiastics, and sanctioned by the presence of the King in full state.

This is doubtless the popular impression of an *auto da fé*, but it is quite erroneous. There was no stake at the *auto* itself. These assemblages were unquestionably of a religious nature, and were conducted by the Inquisitors. Their purpose, however, was primarily not to punish, but to reconcile. Those who, having erred from the faith, had been induced to return to it, made their public recantation, or *auto da fé* ("act of faith"), and having a penance assigned to them, harsh doubtless according to our ideas, but still not that of death, were solemnly absolved and reconciled to the Church. It was in view of this that Mass was sung and sermons preached. The "relaxed" were those who, though at the *auto*, could not be induced to join in it. They were, therefore, after the judgment, not the sentence had been pronounced over them, "relaxed," that is, delivered over to the civil power for sentence and punishment under its arm. The proportion of the "relaxed" to the "penanced" was at all times comparatively small, often very small indeed. Llorente[7] mentions the five *autos* held at Toledo, in 1486, as illustrations of the enormous number of victims, 3,300 in all. Yet out of this large number only 27 were relaxed, and perhaps if he had carried his classification a step further we should have found that a dozen at the most were burnt *alive*. At the two famous *autos* at Valladolid, in 1559, famous because the chief of those which dealt with the Lutherans, out of 71 victims, 26 were relaxed (apparently an unusually large proportion), but 2 only of these were burnt alive. At a public *auto* at Seville, May 29, 1648, we learn from the published *Relacion*, that out of 52 condemned only 1 was relaxed in person, and he, recanting, was garrotted before he was burnt. At the three *autos* at Seville, in 1721, the *Relaciones* give, out of 130 condemned, 27 relaxed and 5 burnt alive. The "relaxation," or deliverance into the hands of the civil officials, accomplished, the latter led away their prisoners either at once, or, more usually, after a day or more's detention in

---

[7] i. 238.

the civil prisons, to the place of public execution. Here the ecclesiastics had no place. They could have no place (except of course that of confessors to the condemned, which is not in question); for to participate in the infliction of capital punishment would have caused them to incur the canonical punishment called "irregularity," which prohibited from performing the functions of the sacred ministry. At these public executions, the King may at times have been present in person, as Philip II. was in 1559. But the *Relacion* of the above-mentioned *auto* at Seville (May 29, 1648) happens to mention the nature of the usual attendance, "Innumerable boys, the troublesome attendants of such criminals, followed the *cortége* to the Quemadero." There had assembled "a numerous multitude on foot, on horse, and in coaches, attracted by the novelty of the spectacle." This reminds us of the assemblages at public executions at Newgate, only that it seems to have been more respectable, and, one would hope, was more deeply sensible of the solemnity of an act of public justice.

Another item in the punishment of the condemned to which exception has been taken, was the confiscation of their goods, an aggravation of the acutest kind to the sufferer, who thus saw those whom he loved best involved in ruin on his account, and a gross injustice to them as the crime was certainly not theirs. To this we may reply that whether confiscation of goods, in view of its effect on the innocent offspring, is an improper punishment to inflict or not, is a question worthy of discussion, and modern opinion appears to solve it in the negative. The practice was, however, universal in former days (there are even some relics of it in the existing laws of England) in the case of treason and felony, crimes with which heresy was considered to be equivalent, and it does not appear why the Inquisition should be chargeable with its adherence to the accepted methods in this particular any more than in that of death by burning. It should, however, in fairness be borne in mind, that the time of grace always allowed and generally extended before the Inquisition began to hold its sessions in a neighbourhood, was specially designed to enable the suspected to avoid confiscation as well as other punishments by timely submission; also that the sovereigns were wont to restore some portion to the widows and orphans if innocent; that the property of the Moriscos was declared not liable to this confiscation, but passed on to the heirs; and finally that the Holy See in its frequent interpositions to secure greater leniency was particularly insistent in protecting the children of the condemned heretics, and thereby became implicated in many disputes with the Spanish sovereigns, who complained of the consequent loss to the royal exchequer.

We have next to consider the charges against the procedure of the Tribunal: so unfair to the accused, who was not allowed to have the name of his accusers or even the exact text of their accusation against him. The fact is, that the facilities for preparing his defence allowed by the Inquisition to the accused, contrast favourably with those allowed in the contemporary civil courts of our own country as well as of the rest of Europe. It has been urged as so hard that the text of the accusation should be altered before being submitted to the accused, and that his accusers should not be confronted with him. The names of the accusers were not given, in order that their identity might be concealed, but the text was only altered in unessentials so far as was necessary to preserve this concealment. On the other hand, in England and elsewhere not the names of the accusers only, but the charges made by them, were concealed from the prisoner's knowledge up to the time of his appearance in court, so that it was quite impossible for him to prepare a carefully thought-out defence. Nor was the English prisoner allowed an advocate at all in criminal cases, whereas the prisoner of the Inquisition was allowed and given one. It is true such an advocate had to be of the number of those in the service of the Inquisition, or at all events must take its oath of secrecy.

This also was a necessity to preserve the secresy about the accusers. But he was under oath to do his best to set forth any truthful defence the accused might have. In the English trials, again, the accused was not allowed to bring forward witnesses on his behalf, whereas in the Inquisition he was, and could even require them to be summoned from the most remote regions. Possibly some readers will be astonished that such unfairness should be imputed to the English system, but that it was so may be read in Sir James Stephen's work already referred to.[8] The notion current in those times was that either the accuser proved his case against the accused, or he failed to prove it. If the latter, a verdict of acquittal was already due and rendered witnesses for the accused unnecessary; if the former, any witness in the contrary sense must either be irrelevant or perjured. That the truth could emerge out of the conflict of opposing testimonies thoroughly sifted, did not enter into the minds of the English and other civil jurists. It was the merit of the Inquisition to have grasped in no small degree the rational principles now realized.

But why should the names of the accusers have been concealed? Could there be any ground for veiling these trials in secresy save to press unfairly on the poor victims? There is a great prejudice in our times against secret trials as pressing unfairly on the accused, but we have occasional reminders that an open trial may also have its disadvantages. To pass over the question of the injury often done to the reputation of third parties, it has occasionally been forced on public attention that crimes cannot be put down, because witnesses know that by giving evidence they expose themselves to great risks, the accused having powerful friends to execute vengeance in their behalf. This was exactly the case with the Inquisition. We have already described the state of affairs in Spain which first caused it to be set in motion. The Maranos and

---

[8] p. 350.

the Moriscos had great power through their wealth, position, and secret bonds of alliance with the unconverted Jews and Moors. These would certainly have endeavoured to neutralize the efforts of the Holy Office had the trials been open. Torquemada, in his Statutes of 1484, gives expressly this defence of secrecy: "It has become notorious that great damage and danger would accrue to the property and person of the witnesses, by the publication of their names, as experience has shown, and still shows, that several of them have been killed, wounded, or maltreated by heretics." The truth about secret trials seems to be that they impose a much greater responsibility on the judges. If a judge is unfair, as we know from history judges have often been, publicity is a valuable check upon them. But as long as the judge is impartial, it is quite possible to work a secret trial in such a manner as to reach a just conclusion, particularly when the court has the power to "inquire," that is, seek out evidence, and is not tied to the mere evidence set before it by others. In the case of inquiries about heresy, there was also this to diminish the otherwise greater difficulties of the secret procedure. Past heresy was of comparatively small account if there was undoubted present orthodoxy, and on this point evidence of a conclusive kind could be furnished on the spot by the accused person if only he chose to furnish it. Provision was of course made by the Inquisition to obviate the chances of unjust accusations and to give the accused every reasonable chance of setting forth his defence. They are provisions obviously dictated by the desire to be impartial and even clement, as well as efficacious. It would take too much space to give them here, but they can be seen in Hefele or more fully in Llorente himself, who, if we separate his facts from his insinuations, is a valuable apologist of the institution he attacks. In the present connexion there is one thing in his pages worthy of special note. In the accounts of many famous processes which he gives, you cannot help feeling that the court invariably succeeds in arriving at the true decision.

Llorente's charge against it is in each case too patently, not that it convicted of heresy those who were not heretics, but that it did not give real heretics sufficient chances of slipping through their hands. It is absurd and illogical to mix up charges. Whether heresy is a crime or not, is one point; whether the law is bound to afford guilty persons facilities for escaping justice is another. On the former we have already offered some remarks; as to the latter, one would imagine no remarks were needed.

The next charge against the Inquisition is its use of torture. We are all agreed that the practice is cruel and happily obsolete. But again, why is the Inquisition to be more blameworthy than other European courts of the period? Torture was everywhere in use whilst it was in use with the Inquisition, and became obsolete there when it grew into disfavour elsewhere. It is indeed the boast of English lawyers that it was never a part of the English procedure, and this is true of the ordinary procedure. But it was employed in England nevertheless, under the prerogative of the Crown, particularly during the Tudor and early Stuart period. "Under Henry VIII. it appears to have been in frequent use. Only two cases occurred under Edward VI., and eight under Mary. The reign of Elizabeth was its culminating point. In the words of Hallam, 'The rack seldom stood idle in the Tower during the latter part of Elizabeth's reign.'"[9] And we may add incidentally that while Edward and Mary do not appear to have employed it in cases of heresy, Elizabeth employed it ordinarily and ruthlessly against the Catholics. If, too, in England torture was not employed under the ordinary procedure, Sir James Stephen tells us[10] this was merely because the ordinary procedure had slight scruples about convicting on very insufficient evidence. Torture was employed by the Inquisition, as by other courts, in order to

---

[9] *Encycl. Brit.* s.v. "Torture."
[10] Op. cit. i. 222.

extract evidence which could not be otherwise verified, and so obtain the certainty, if it existed, without which no conviction was possible. In short, if we are to compare the Inquisition with other contemporary courts whether in Spain or England or elsewhere, in regard to the employment of torture, the result must be to award the Inquisition the palm of greater mercy. It limited largely the number of those who could inflict it, permitted its infliction only when the evidence against the prisoner amounted already to a *semi-plena probatio* (*i.e.* nearly complete proof), permitted it only once in each case, and required the presence of the inquisitor and the ordinary, not, as is popularly thought, to gloat over the agonies of the sufferer, but to see that the experiment was conducted with as much mercy and mildness as was possible under the conditions. These precautions do not seem to have existed in the same degree in England.

In like manner the charge of inhumanity against the dungeons of the Inquisition needs only to be dealt with by the comparative method in order to melt away. Is the story told, only a century ago, by John Howard and Elizabeth Fry, as to the state of English and continental prisons so completely forgotten? Doubtless the prison cells of the past were in flagrant opposition to the dictates of humanity, and one can only marvel that they could last so long without encountering the protests of the merciful. The Inquisition was naturally governed in this respect also by contemporary methods, though analogy would lead us to surmise that here too it was to some extent in advance of its age. One thing at least we may hope, that it had no dungeon like that into which, under Elizabeth, Father Sherwood was put in the Tower of London. This we learn from Jardine, "was a cell below high-water mark and totally dark; and, as the tide flowed, innumerable rats which infested the muddy banks of the Thames were driven through the crevices of the walls into the dungeons."[11] Alarm was the least part of the torture to the terrified inmates. At times flesh was torn from the arms and legs of the prisoners during sleep by these rats. And this was after a century of enlightenment had separated a new age from that of Torquemada. We have Llorente's unimpeachable testimony for the improvement that had set in by the commencement of the present century. At that time he tells us the cells were "good vaulted chambers well lighted and dry," and "large enough for exercise." Nor were chains in use, unless perhaps in an isolated case to prevent suicide.[12]{n12} As much could not have been said of the generality of English prisons at that date.

The last charge relates to the manner of the arrests. That the Inquisition established an all-embracing system of *espionnage* through the agency of secret officials called "familiars" is an important feature in the Protestant conception of its methods. But the "familiars" were not a secret body. They were a sort of militia containing a large number, perhaps a majority, of religious-minded, influential persons. The purpose of their enrolment as such was not to spy out heresies, but to constitute an organized fund of physical force in support of the tribunal against the very considerable power of the heretics it was endeavouring to over-master. They had a large part in the conduct of the *autos da fé*, and apparently the officials, apparitors, &c., of the court were of their number. But there is no ground for thinking them to be mysterious beings with cat-like tread such as a morbid fancy has depicted them. Arrests were perhaps at times made in secresy. This is usual and according to common sense when otherwise an arrest might be successfully impeded. But that after arrest, no news of what had happened were allowed to transpire, or a word of allusion to the occurrence to be made, is absurd. As soon as an arrest was

---

[11] Cf. Jardine's *Readings on the use of Torture in England*.
[12] i. p. 300.

made, an official of the court was at once sent to the prisoner's house to take an inventory of his possessions. How could this be done and the family remain in ignorance of what had happened? That all conversation about the arrests made was forbidden seems also altogether improbable, and at least requires to be established by proof, not imagination. At the best, there may be this slight ground for the notion. To manifest sympathy with the heresy, not the person, of the prisoner, would be to repeat the fault of which he was suspected, and to incur its liabilities. In all cases, when a criminal has been carried off by justice, it is prudent for his accomplices to observe reticence.

No other charge occurs to us demanding notice in a short pamphlet, but readers who desire fuller information may be referred to Hefele's excellent chapters on the subject in his *Life of Cardinal Ximenez*. All that now remains for us here is to correct the notion that the Holy See is responsible for the excesses of the Spanish Inquisition. It is disputed among authorities whether the tribunal ought not to be regarded as a royal rather than a papal court, and Bishop Hefele is strongly of this view. The inquisitors were, however, unquestionably ecclesiastics, and drew their jurisdiction from Papal Bulls. In this sense the court was certainly Papal, but the appointments were all made by the Crown, and the Crown, not the Pope, is responsible for the harshness. The Papal power of control, though theoretically absolute, was practically small. The Popes met with constant opposition from the Spanish monarchs in all their attempts to interpose. They did, however, interpose frequently, both by protests, by threats of excommunication, by drawing to themselves appeals, and sometimes by revising largely in the sense of mercy or even altogether remitting sentences passed by the tribunal. We are dependent for our information concerning this matter on Llorente, who alone has had access to the Papal Letters. He gives us some letters of expostulation written by Sixtus IV., and these exhibit this Pope just as we should expect to find a Pope, anxious to put down heresy, and therefore granting the spiritual faculties solicited by the sovereigns for their nominees, and even exhorting them to zeal in their work; but at the same time desirous that the zeal should be tempered by mercy, and deeply incensed when he discovered that the claims of mercy were so disregarded. It is the voice of genuine compassion which speaks out in terms like these, "Since it is clemency which, as far as is possible to human nature, makes men equal to God, We ask and entreat the King and Queen by the tender mercies of our Lord Jesus Christ to imitate Him whose property it is ever to show mercy and to spare, and so to spare the citizens of Seville and its diocese," &c. Nor did Sixtus stay at words. First he appointed the Archbishop of Seville as a judge of appeal, and, when this arrangement failed of its effect, he allowed the victims to carry appeals to Rome, where already they had fled in large numbers, hopeful of obtaining, as they did obtain, either complete absolution or a large alleviation of their penance from that merciful tribunal. Surely it is a significant fact that fugitives from the harshness of the Spanish Inquisition should have thought of Rome as the best refuge to which they could flee. Succeeding Popes are stated by Llorente to have made similar endeavours to mitigate the extreme severities of the inquisitors. They were, however, invariably foiled by the Spanish sovereigns, who had the power in their hands.

Llorente tries to take the edge off these remonstrances of the Holy See by insinuating that they sprang from the base motive of cupidity; that the Popes had an eye to the fees they could extort as the price of their absolutions. But this is mere insinuation for which there is not a shadow of proof. The action of the Popes in regard to the Inquisition is quite in keeping with the character that has always been theirs. The Popes as individuals have had their personal qualities. Some have been sterner, others milder, in their temperament and in their rule. But the Holy See has all along stood out among the thrones of Christendom conspicuous for its love of mercy and tenderness towards the erring and the suffering.

And not the Holy See only, but the clergy also, if we take them as a body. As the ministers of Jesus Christ, more entirely devoted to His service and more exclusively occupied with the study of His Life, this is what would be expected of them. And what honest historian of the past, or observer of the present, can deny that the expectation has been realized? It was the clergy, in the wild middle ages, who were the refuge of the weak and oppressed against the lawless monarchs and chieftains: it was they who originated charitable institutions under so many forms. And in our own days, they are engaged everywhere in exactly the same work. This does not mean, that the Catholic laity are backward in charitable enterprises. It means only that the clergy are wont to be the leaders in such works. Surely then it is reasonable to judge of their part in the Inquisition by these analogies, and this is all we have been contending for. The Inquisition belonged to an age which was far harsher in dealing with crime than our own, and the clergy are always, necessarily, imbued with the ideas and feelings that are in the air they breathe. We ought not to be surprised to find that when they acted as Inquisitors, they adopted methods prevalent in their age, which to us seem harsh and revolting. But we should expect also that their judicial behaviour would in some sort reflect the tender-heartedness in all other respects demonstratively characteristic of their body. In a word, the faults which we deplore in these Inquisitors were the faults of their age, which happily has passed away. The redeeming qualities we discover in them were the virtues natural to their state. The latter survive, and we may hope, ripen, and they furnish a guarantee which should give satisfaction to terrified Protestants, that our return to power, if so unlikely a thing should be in the near future, will not bring with it any danger to their lives and liberties.

It will be convenient to sum up what has been established in a few propositions.

1. The intolerance of Catholics consists in this that they believe our Lord has made His revelation sufficiently clear for all men to recognize it if they will. Still, modern Catholics have no desire to coerce those who will not recognize it. The tolerance of Protestants consists in this that they believe every one must be left to his private judgment in a matter so obscure as the true religion. But they persecute those whose private judgment recommends them to become Catholics.

2. No one wants back the Spanish Inquisition, but although following the notions of its age, it put to death altogether a very large number of heretics, the English civil courts put to death many more for lesser crimes—like sheep-stealing.

3. Torture employed by the Inquisition in conformity with the common law of Spain, but with greater restrictions. Torture employed in England much more fiercely, in spite of the common law of England. The culminating point of its use in England was under Elizabeth, who inflicted it ruthlessly on Catholics.

4. Names of accusers for their security concealed in Spain from the accused, but the accusation given him and the assistance of an advocate. No advocates allowed in English criminal trials of former days, and accusations not shown to the accused till he came into court.

5. Inquisition dungeons probably never worse than contemporary English dungeons, and certainly much better in the latter days of its existence.

6. The victims of the Inquisition had such a belief in the humanity of the Popes that they fled to his territory and begged to have their cases judged there.

www.ingramcontent.com/pod-product-compliance
Lightning Source LLC
Chambersburg PA
CBHW060552030426
42337CB00019B/3530